Facts About the Okapi

By Lisa Strattin

© 2019 Lisa Strattin

FREE BOOK

FREE FOR ALL SUBSCRIBERS

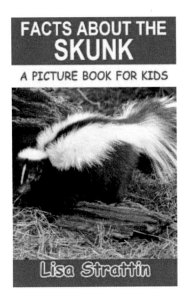

LisaStrattin.com/Subscribe-Here

BOX SET

- **FACTS ABOUT THE POISON DART FROGS**
- **FACTS ABOUT THE THREE TOED SLOTH**
- **FACTS ABOUT THE RED PANDA**
- **FACTS ABOUT THE SEAHORSE**
- **FACTS ABOUT THE PLATYPUS**
- **FACTS ABOUT THE REINDEER**
- **FACTS ABOUT THE PANTHER**
- **FACTS ABOUT THE SIBERIAN HUSKY**

LisaStrattin.com/BookBundle

Facts for Kids Picture Books by Lisa Strattin

Little Blue Penguin, Vol 92

Chipmunk, Vol 5

Frilled Lizard, Vol 39

Blue and Gold Macaw, Vol 13

Poison Dart Frogs, Vol 50

Blue Tarantula, Vol 115

African Elephants, Vol 8

Amur Leopard, Vol 89

Sabre Tooth Tiger, Vol 167

Baboon, Vol 174

Sign Up for New Release Emails Here

LisaStrattin.com/subscribe-here

All information in this book has been carefully researched and checked for factual accuracy. However, the author and publisher makes no warranty, express or implied, that the information contained herein is appropriate for every individual, situation or purpose and assume no responsibility for errors or omissions. The reader assumes the risk and full responsibility for all actions, and the author will not be held responsible for any loss or damage, whether consequential, incidental, special or otherwise, that may result from the information presented in this book.

All images are free for use or purchased from stock photo sites or royalty free for commercial use.

Some coloring pages might be of the general species due to lack of available images.

I have relied on my own observations as well as many different sources for this book and I have done my best to check facts and give credit where it is due. In the event that any material is used without proper permission, please contact me so that the oversight can be corrected.

COVER IMAGE

https://www.flickr.com/photos/cuatrok77/13129901383/

ADDITIONAL IMAGES

https://www.flickr.com/photos/jeades/569603387/

https://www.flickr.com/photos/15016964@N02/3878057347/

https://www.flickr.com/photos/pahudson/4758469803/

https://www.flickr.com/photos/huhnbeauftragter/8549374466/

https://www.flickr.com/photos/markhadley/859300722/

https://www.flickr.com/photos/cowlet/3656890320/

https://www.flickr.com/photos/zooeurope/21901912419/

https://www.flickr.com/photos/ekilby/8492580965/

https://www.flickr.com/photos/chrisinphilly5448/2340893209/

https://www.flickr.com/photos/sittinginthekitchensink/4579420354/

Contents

INTRODUCTION

The Okapi lives in Africa in a small tropical mountain forest range. Even though they look like deer, they are closely related to the giraffe!

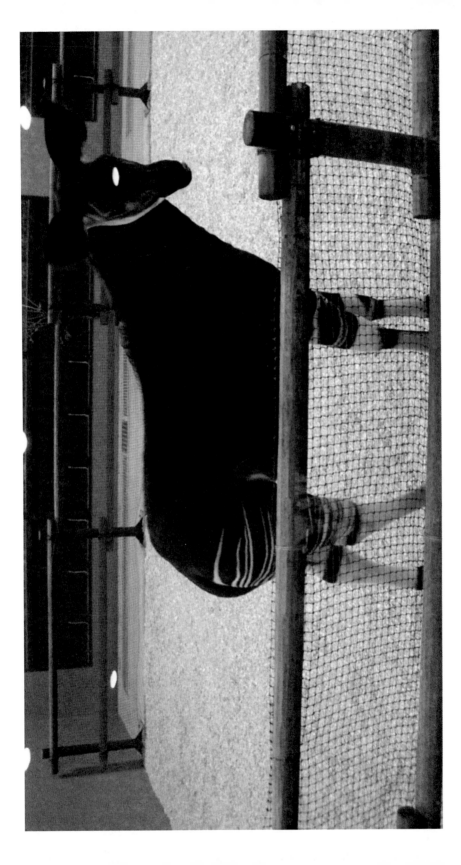

BEHAVIOR

The Okapi is an animal that is most active during the day. They like to roam around paths in their home range looking for food. They spend much of their life alone except when the females are taking care of their calves. They get along with other Okapi when they eat together, but only for a short time. They really would rather be alone.

The males will fight one another over specific territories and sometimes over the female that they have chosen to mate.

They have been called the "Forest Zebra."

APPEARANCE

The Okapi has a long neck that helps them get to leaves far above the ground. Their fur is a reddish-brown, with long white stripes on their back end and at the tops of their legs. These markings help the Okapi to hide in the forest where it lives, it provides a camouflage for them. They have white ankles and a dark muzzle. They have a very long, black tongue. They are one of very few animals in the world that is able to lick their own ears!

REPRODUCTION

The female Okapi is pregnant for as long as 16 months before she gives birth to one calf. The calf is able to stand on all four legs within an hour from birth! The mother protects her calf, keeping her in a safe nesting spot and watching for danger. She nurses the calf for about 6 months to a year. The calf will start eating grasses and other vegetative food at around 6 months, even though the calf might nurse from the mother for a longer time.

LIFE SPAN

Most Okapis live for 20 to 30 years!

SIZE

The adult Okapi can be from 5 to 6 feet long and weigh up to 650 pounds!

HABITAT

The Okapi only lives in the tropical rainforests of the African Republic of Congo. They are shy animals that hide from people and other animals in the thick forest. They usually are near some slow-moving rivers so that they have a fresh water source. This water helps keep the vegetation that they like to eat plentiful in their natural forest range.

DIET

The Okapi eats only plants. They will eat twigs, leaves, shoots, and berries. With their long tongue, they are able to reach up into the trees to grab whatever is growing there! Some of the plants they eat is poisonous to humans! They sometimes eat the red clay on the forest floor in order to get the salt and minerals they need to stay healthy.

ENEMIES

There are not many natural enemies of the Okapi. The mainly have to watch out for Leopards which will pounce on them for a meal. The Okapi's hearing is very acute which allows them to hear the animals on the ground, but the Leopard is stealthy and can sneak up on them.

SUITABILITY AS PETS

The Okapi has been kept as a farm animal in some animals. Of course, they are too big to be house pets, but some ranches and farms keep them and treat them as pets.

If you want to see them, you can probably see some in zoos where there is a suitable habitat built for them.

COLOR ME

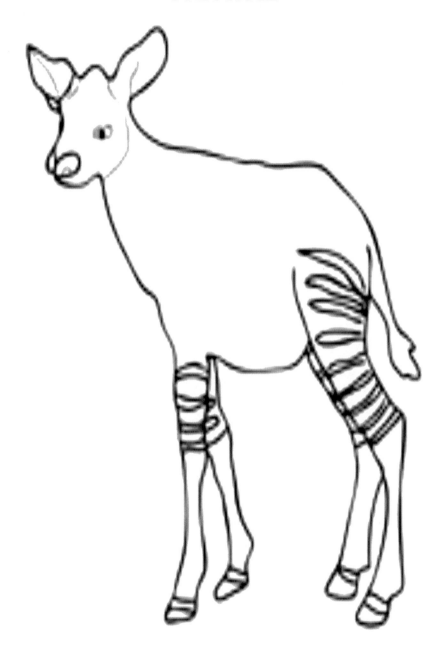

COLOR ME

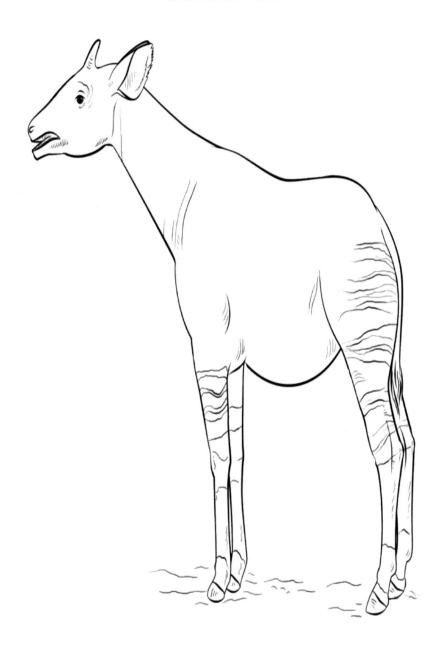

COLOR ME

COLOR ME

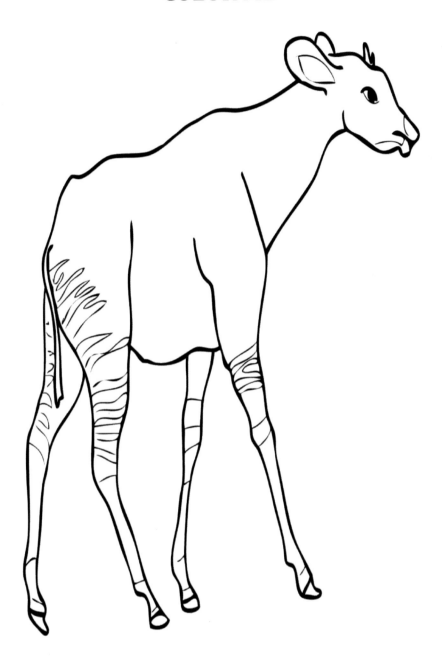

COLOR ME

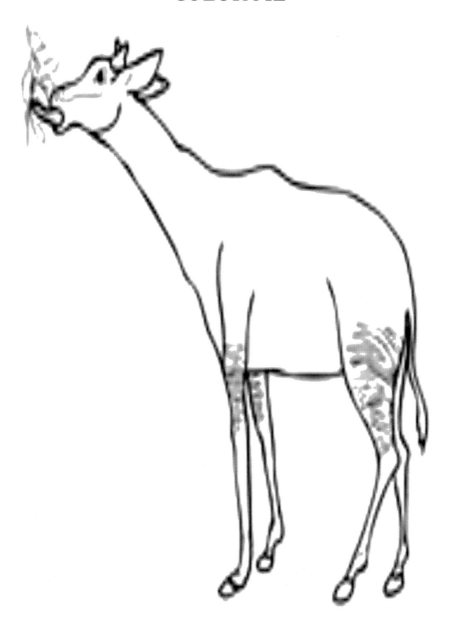

COLOR ME

COLOR ME

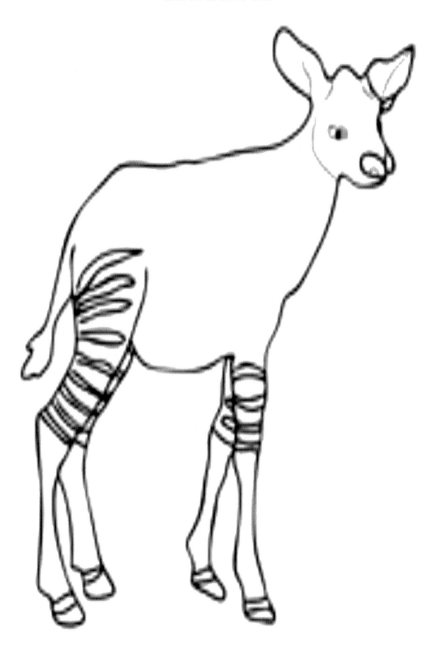

COLOR ME

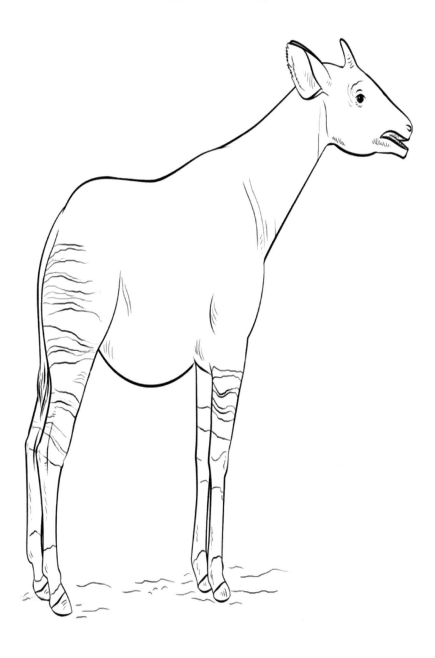

COLOR ME

COLOR ME

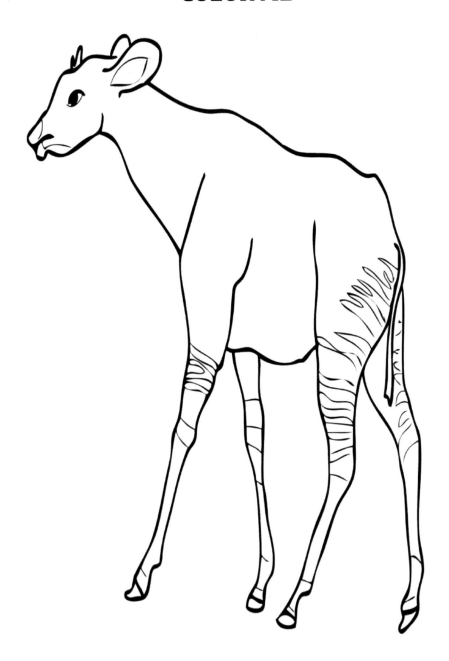

Please leave me a review here:

LisaStrattin.com/Review-Vol-336

For more Kindle Downloads Visit Lisa Strattin
Author Page on Amazon Author Central

amazon.com/author/lisastrattin

To see upcoming titles, visit my website at
LisaStrattin.com– most books available on Kindle!

LisaStrattin.com

FREE BOOK

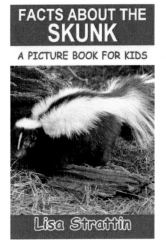

Made in the USA
Middletown, DE
15 December 2022

18602433R00024